NOW THAT I AM BAP...

A PUZZLE ...
FOR LDS KI...

Arie Van De Graaff

to Parker

Walnut Springs Press, LLC
110 South 800 West
Brigham City, Utah 84302
http://walnutspringspress.blogspot.com

Copyright © 2010 by Arie Van De Graaff

ISBN: 978-1-935217-44-2

Getting Ready for Baptism

MEET MOLLY AND PETER. THEY ARE BOTH TURNING EIGHT YEARS OLD AND ARE GETTING READY TO BE BAPTIZED. FOLLOW THEM THROUGH THIS BOOK AS THEY LEARN ABOUT SERVICE AFTER BAPTISM, EXAMPLES FROM THE SCRIPTURES, THE ARTICLES OF FAITH, AND MISSIONARY WORK. BUT FIRST, THEY NEED YOUR HELP GETTING READY FOR THEIR BAPTISMS. YOU CAN BEGIN BY FINDING EIGHT THINGS IN COMMON WITH MOLLY'S ROOM AND PETER'S ROOM BELOW.

Peter is celebrating his eighth birthday, which means he'll soon be baptized! See if you can find ten differences between the two pictures.

It's Molly's eighth birthday. See how many sets of eight you can find in this picture.

In Primary CTR classes, you are taught the things you need to know to be baptized. See if you can find the letters C, T, and R four times each in this picture.

Each of these children is getting baptized, but that isn't the only thing they have in common. Each child in every row of three—either vertical, horizontal, or diagonal—has something in common with the other children in the row. Can you identify what they have in common?

A. _____ B. _____ C. _____ D. _____

E. _____ F. _____ G. _____ H. _____

Jesus taught that the two great commandments are to love God and love our _____.
Follow the instructions below to find out whom else we should love.

LOOK AT THE WORD IN EACH CIRCLE. FIND THE PICTURE IN THE CIRCLE
THAT BEGINS WITH THE FIRST LETTER IN THE WORD. DRAW A LINE FROM
THAT PICTURE TO THE PICTURE THAT BEGINS WITH THE SECOND LETTER
IN THE WORD. CONTINUE TO THE END. DRAW A LINE FROM THE LAST
PICTURE TO THE FIRST. LOOK AT THE SHAPE THAT WAS CREATED.

LOVE

GOD

CROSS OUT ANY SHAPE
BELOW THAT WASN'T
CREATED ABOVE, THEN
WRITE THE LEFTOVER
LETTERS TO GET YOUR
ANSWER.

___ ___ ___ ___ ___ ___ ___

S N T I A G H F B O L R

8

Each of the kids in this picture is wearing or holding something in common with another. For example, in the bottom left-hand corner, the girl has the same paintbrush as the boy next to her. Now find something that boy has in common with another child in the picture and so on, to discover the secret message. It's a message that will make us and the people around us happy.

SECRET MESSAGE:

H E __ __ __   __ __ __ __ __

9

To find out what type of interview this boy is going to have with his bishop, follow the directions below.

MATCH THE SQUARES BELOW WITH THE SAME SQUARES IN THE PICTURE ABOVE. WRITE THE LETTERS FOR EACH SQUARE ON THE SPACE BELOW, THE LETTER ON THE SIDE FIRST AND THE LETTER ON TOP SECOND, TO GET YOUR ANSWER. (CAREFUL, SOME OF THE SQUARES ARE UPSIDE DOWN.)

_ _ _ _ _ _ _ _ _

INTERVIEW

Peter's mother wants to buy a tie for him to wear after his baptism. Each row is missing at least one tie. To figure out which tie goes on each shirt without a tie, look at the pattern in each row. Then write the letter associated with each missing tie in the space at the bottom of the page to find out which tie pattern Peter's mom chooses.

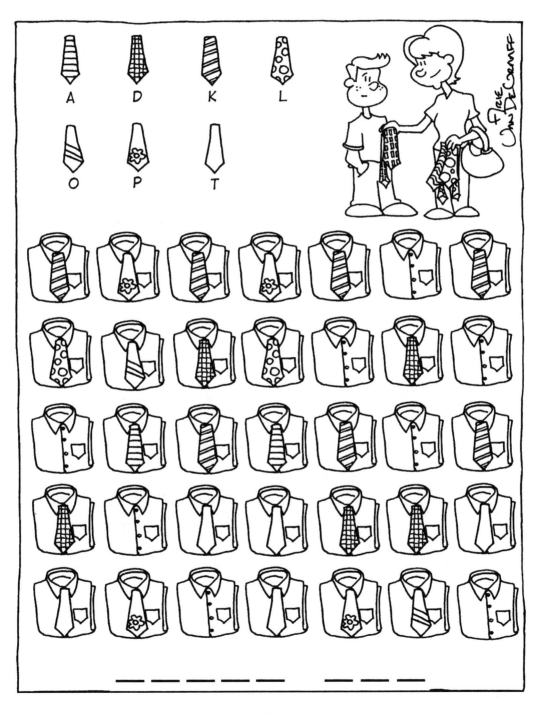

Molly's grandma wants to buy Molly a piece of jewelry with "CTR" on it to remind her after her baptism to always choose the right. Figure out which piece of jewelry she buys by identifying the one you can follow from Molly's grandmother to Molly.

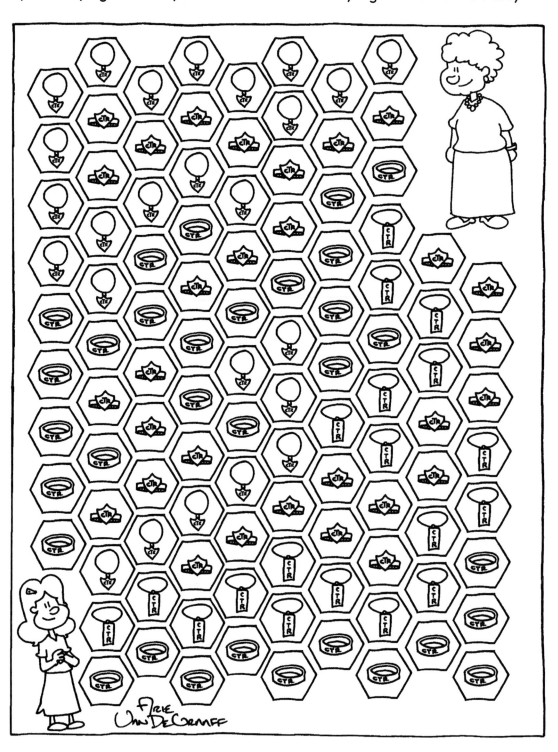

Molly wants to personalize the invitations to her baptism that she is sending out to her friends and family. See if you can match each envelope with the picture of the person the envelope is going to.

To find out what Peter's family is doing for family home evening to get ready for his baptism, follow the instructions below.

MATCH THE SQUARES BELOW WITH THE SAME SQUARES IN THE PICTURE ABOVE. WRITE THE LETTERS FOR EACH SQUARE ON THE SPACE BELOW, THE LETTER ON THE SIDE FIRST AND THE LETTER ON TOP SECOND, TO GET YOUR ANSWER. (CAREFUL, SOME OF THE SQUARES ARE UPSIDE DOWN.)

___ ___ ___ ___ ___ ___ ___ ___

Peter needs to eat a good breakfast because today is a special day. Find out what's happening today by first identifying which letters are not in Peter's bowl of cereal and then unscrambling those letters into a word.

___ __ _____

Molly's cousins and her aunt and uncle are excited to attend her baptism, but they need help figuring out where to sit in their minivan. Can you figure out their seating arrangements by using the clues below?

FAMILY MEMBERS:

A. DAD
B. MOM
C. AVA
D. TESS
E. LEAH
F. WILL
G. GABE
H. TY

CLUES:

- ✔ DAD LIKES TO DRIVE.
- ✔ MOM GETS CARSICK IN THE BACK.
- ✔ TY NEEDS AVA TO SIT NEXT TO HIM TO HELP HIM.
- ✔ WILL AND TY ARE IN CHILD CARSEATS (3 AND 4).
- ✔ TESS AND GABE CANNOT SIT NEXT TO EACH OTHER.
- ✔ GABE NEEDS TO SIT BEHIND A CARSEAT FOR EXTRA LEG SPACE.

SEATING ORDER:

1. _____   5. _____

2. _____   6. _____

3. _____   7. _____

4. _____   8. _____

Molly is helping her mother prepare for a party after her baptism. Each row is missing one or more snack. Looking at the pattern in each row, figure out which snack goes on which empty plate. To find out which relative is likely to eat the most food at the party, write the letter associated with each missing snack on the space provided at the bottom of the page.

Peter's and Molly's families are posing for a photo at their baptism. Try to find all the hidden objects in this picture.

BANANA   BASEBALL BAT   CRAYON   DONUT   DRUMSTICK   DUCK   FISHING POLE   KITE

PAINTBRUSH   PAPER CLIP   PENCIL   PIZZA   RULER   SALT SHAKER   SCREW   TOOTHBRUSH

Molly is ready to get baptized. See if you can find ten differences between the two pictures.

When someone is confirmed a member of the Church, he or she receives the gift of the Holy Ghost. The Holy Ghost fulfills a number of roles. To find out what one of His roles is, follow the directions below.

LOOK AT THE WORD IN EACH CIRCLE. FIND THE PICTURE IN THE CIRCLE THAT BEGINS WITH THE FIRST LETTER IN THE WORD. DRAW A LINE FROM THAT PICTURE TO THE PICTURE THAT BEGINS WITH THE SECOND LETTER IN THE WORD. CONTINUE TO THE END. DRAW A LINE FROM THE LAST PICTURE TO THE FIRST. LOOK AT THE SHAPE THAT WAS CREATED.

HOLY

GHOST

CROSS OUT ANY SHAPE BELOW THAT WASN'T CREATED ABOVE, THEN WRITE THE LEFTOVER LETTERS TO GET YOUR ANSWER.

C E ☆ S M ☆ L O ☆ A ☆ E S R

Now That I Am Baptized

IN THE BOOK OF MORMON, NEPHI CALLS BAPTISM A GATE. IN A LOT OF WAYS THAT GATE ISN'T THE END, BUT THE BEGINNING OF OUR WORK. BEHIND HER GRANDMA'S GATE, MOLLY IS DOING SOME WORK OF HER OWN. FIND OUT WHAT KIND OF WORK SHE'S DOING BY MATCHING BOTH THE RIGHT AND LEFT SIDES OF EACH FLOWER AND ADDING THE NUMBERS FROM EACH SIDE. MATCH THE NUMBER OF THE FLOWERS WITH THE LETTERS ON THE FENCE POSTS AND WRITE THOSE LETTERS IN THE SPACES BELOW.

We are blessed by the priesthood throughout our lives. Match just a few of the blessings of the priesthood with the timeline of this girl's life.

Each square in the quilt these girls are tying has something in common with another square. The square with the star in it has the same background pattern as a square with a circle in it. To learn the name of the Primary program that girls begin when they turn eight, find the square that has something in common with that square.

SECRET MESSAGE:

A C _ _ _ _ _ _ _   _ _ _ _

In many parts of the world, boys who turn eight not only can be baptized, but they can also participate in Cub Scouts. These Cub Scouts are racing pinewood cars. See which car reaches the finish line first by finding the car that you can follow from the Cub Scouts to the checkered flag.

Being a member of the Church means being willing to help teach other members—even as a Primary student. Can you find the two identical pictures below of a boy sharing a talk in Primary?

Each person in this picture is holding or wearing something in common with another person. For example, the person at the podium is wearing the same watch as the man on the front row. Now find out what the man on the front row has in common with someone else and so on, to discover what else all the people share.

SECRET MESSAGE:

<u>T</u> <u>E</u> __ __ __ __ __ __ __ __ __ __ __

26

To find out why this little girl is counting out her money, move the number of spaces indicated by each arrow and write down the letter on each stack of coins you stop at, in the spaces provided. Start at the stack of coins with a star.

Members of the Church are encouraged to go without food or drink one day each month, usually the first Sunday. This is called fasting, and it can be difficult the first few times you try it. To see which meal the boy in this picture is excited to eat at the end of his fast, find the two plates that match.

When worthy boys who have been baptized turn twelve, they can receive the Aaronic Priesthood. One responsibility that comes with the Aaronic Priesthood is collecting fast offerings from the members of the Church. Help these two deacons follow the directions to get to the home where they need to collect fast offerings.

START AT "A"

Part of being a Church member is accepting callings to serve in the Church. Match each member below with his or her calling.

As members of the Church, we should always try to be nice to everyone. In these two pictures, a boy is inviting a new student to eat with him. See if you can find ten differences between the pictures.

Being a member of the Church means serving your family. Help this girl find her little brother's missing Darkguy action figure.

Temples are holy buildings where worthy members of the Church make covenants with Heavenly Father. Match each temple with the date it was dedicated.

Provo Temple

Swiss Temple

Draper Temple

Salt Lake Temple

Jordan River Temple

St George Temple

April 1877

April 1893

September 1955

February 1972

November 1981

March 2009

In the Book of Mormon, Lehi dreamed of an iron rod that represented the word of God. The iron rod led to the tree of life. To find out what we should do with the word of God so we can enjoy the fruit of the tree of life, follow the directions below.

MATCH THE SQUARES BELOW WITH THE SAME SQUARES IN THE PICTURE ABOVE. WRITE THE LETTERS FOR EACH SQUARE ON THE SPACE BELOW, THE LETTER ON THE SIDE FIRST AND THE LETTER ON TOP SECOND, TO GET YOUR ANSWER. (CAREFUL, SOME OF THE SQUARES ARE UPSIDE DOWN.)

Each candy bar in this display has something in common with another candy bar. For example, the bar in the top left corner has the same pattern as the one that is second to the bottom on the right. Now find out what that candy bar has in common with another and so on, to discover what the boy on the left understands would be broken by stealing.

SECRET MESSAGE:

C O _ _ _ _ _ _ _ _ _ _ _

Uh-oh! This boy is eating a cookie his mother was saving for something else. To find out what he needs to do next, move the number of spaces indicated by each arrow and write down the letter on each cookie you stop at, in the spaces provided.

This family is doing nothing wrong in watching General Conference together, but there are ten things wrong with this picture. Can you find them all?

Baptism is only the first covenant (promise) that Church members make with Heavenly Father. Other covenants are made in the temple. Find the hidden objects in this picture.

BANANA   BASEBALL   BRUSH   CARROT   DUCK   MUG   NUT   PAINTBRUSH   PENCIL

PIZZA SLICE   SALT SHAKER   SCREWDRIVER   SPOON   TOOTHBRUSH   WATCH   WATERMELON

Scripture and Church History Stories

IN THE SCRIPTURES AND THROUGHOUT CHURCH HISTORY, THERE ARE EXAMPLES OF RIGHTEOUS LIVING. WE CAN READ ABOUT HEROES WHO BRAVELY CHOSE THE RIGHT AND SACRIFICED MUCH FOR THE GOSPEL. WE CAN ALSO LEARN WHAT OUR HEAVENLY FATHER WOULD HAVE US DO TO RETURN TO LIVE WITH HIM. PETER IS TRYING TO DRESS UP LIKE A PROPHET FROM THE SCRIPTURES, BUT HE'S MISSING HIS HAT. SEE IF YOU CAN HELP HIM FIND A PROPER HAT BY CIRCLING THE ONE THAT MATCHES HIS OUTFIT.

In order to baptize people, Joseph Smith had to receive the authority from someone holding the Aaronic Priesthood. On May 15, 1829, John the Baptist conferred that priesthood upon Joseph Smith and Oliver Cowdery on the bank of the Susquehanna River. Find the hidden objects in this picture.

BANANA   CARROT   CELL PHONE   ICE CREAM   JUMP ROPE   MITTEN   ORANGE

PAPER CLIP   PEAR   PENCIL   SPOON   STARFISH   STRAW   TEA CUP   TIE   TOOTHBRUSH

Because he grew up in the desert, John the Baptist had an interesting diet. The Bible says that John ate two of the following: berries, bread, fish, honey, locust, nuts, and oranges. To find out the two foods he ate, see which items lead him to the River Jordan.

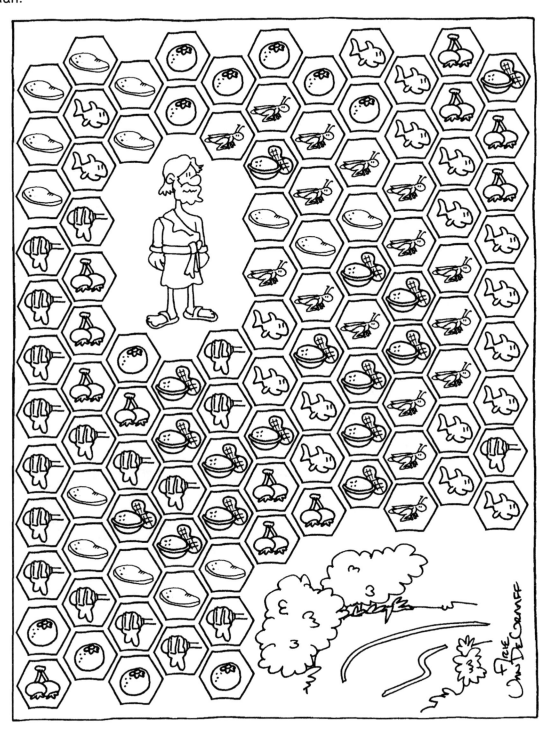

While hiding from the wicked King Noah, Alma taught the people and baptized them in the Waters of Mormon. Find a path through the current to Alma.

Use the grid to redraw the mixed-up picture to see the form in which the Holy Ghost manifested Himself at Christ's baptism.

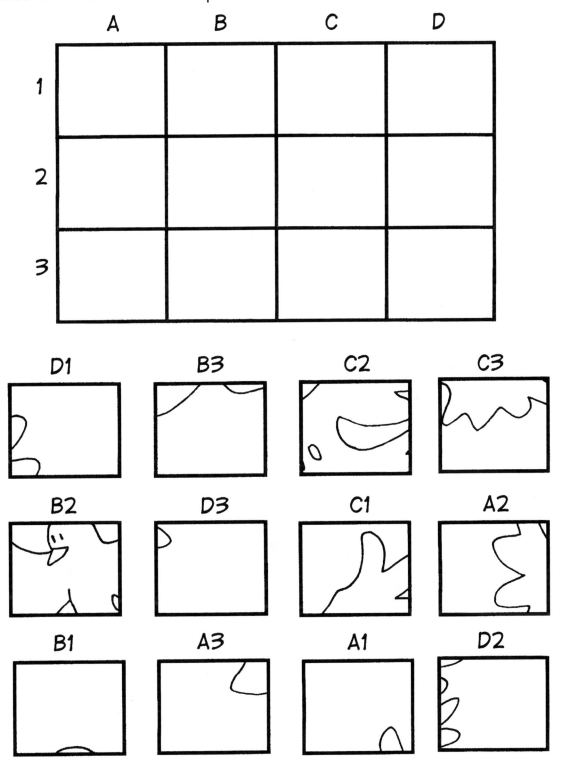

Each of the Book of Mormon heroes below is a good example of how we should follow Christ, but that is not all they share. Every row of three—either vertical, horizontal, or diagonal—has something in common. Can you identify what the heroes in each row have in common?

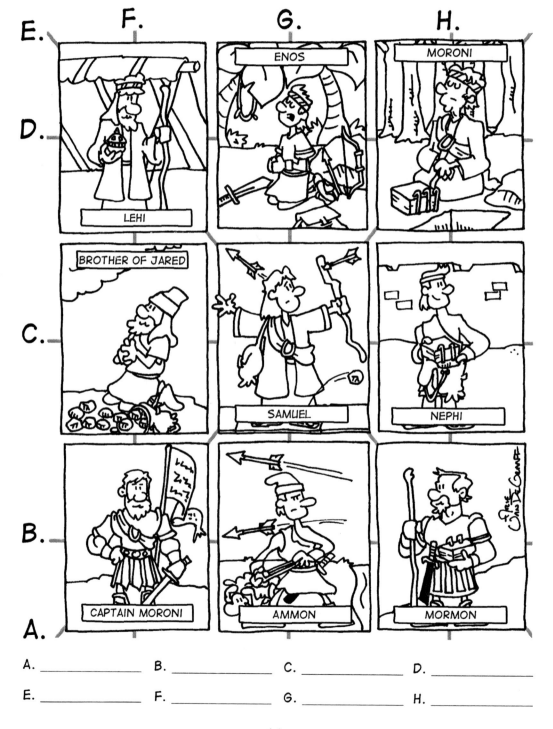

A. _____ B. _____ C. _____ D. _____

E. _____ F. _____ G. _____ H. _____

In the Book of Mormon, Captain Moroni built large walls around the Nephite cities to protect the people from their enemies. As members of the Church today, we should build spiritual walls to protect ourselves from sin. Find the hidden objects in this picture.

BANANA   BASEBALL   CANDLE   CARROT   COLANDER   FORK   ICE CREAM   LIGHT BULB

PAINTBRUSH   PAPER CLIP   PENCIL   PIECE OF CAKE   PRETZEL   SCREW   TEA CUP   WATCH

After he received the gold plates, which he would later translate into the Book of Mormon, Joseph Smith bravely protected them from evil men who wanted to steal them. Help Joseph get the plates out of the woods while avoiding the would-be thieves.

A keystone is an important piece of an arch that holds all the other pieces in place. To find out what Joseph Smith called "the keystone of our religion," follow the instructions below.

LOOK AT THE WORD IN EACH CIRCLE. FIND THE PICTURE IN THE CIRCLE THAT BEGINS WITH THE FIRST LETTER IN THE WORD. DRAW A LINE FROM THAT PICTURE TO THE PICTURE THAT BEGINS WITH THE SECOND LETTER IN THE WORD. CONTINUE TO THE END. DRAW A LINE FROM THE LAST PICTURE TO THE FIRST. LOOK AT THE SHAPE THAT WAS CREATED.

KEY

STONE

CROSS OUT ANY SHAPE BELOW THAT WASN'T CREATED ABOVE, THEN WRITE THE LEFT OVER LETTERS TO GET YOUR ANSWER.

B O S O E K O F T M O R R M A O N

Naaman, a leper in the Old Testament, wanted to be healed. The prophet Elisha told him to bathe in the River Jordan seven times. At first, Naaman didn't want to do this simple thing, but when he had faith and did as the prophet told him to do, Naaman was healed from his leprosy. We also need to show faith by doing the simple things. Can you find the two images of Naaman that are the same?

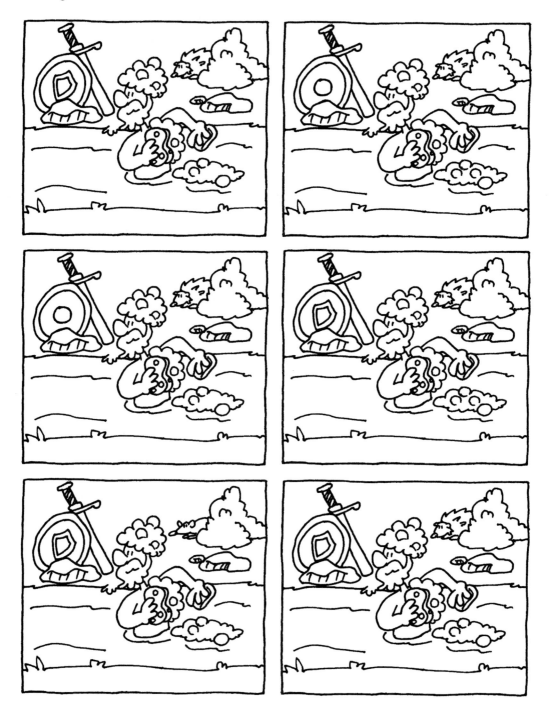

Samuel was a young man when he was lying in bed and heard the voice of the Lord call him to be a prophet. We can hear the still, small voice when we are doing what is right. Can you find ten things that don't belong in Samuel's Old Testament bedroom?

Nephi showed his faith by his actions. The pictures of the story of Nephi breaking his bow are all out of order. In the upper left-hand corner of each picture, write the order (from 1 to 6) of each picture. If you need help, read the story in 1 Nephi 16:18–31.

In Lehi's dream of the tree of life, the iron rod led people to the tree. To keep the promises we make when we are baptized, we must also hold on to the iron rod. To find out what the iron rod stood for in Lehi's dream, follow the directions below.

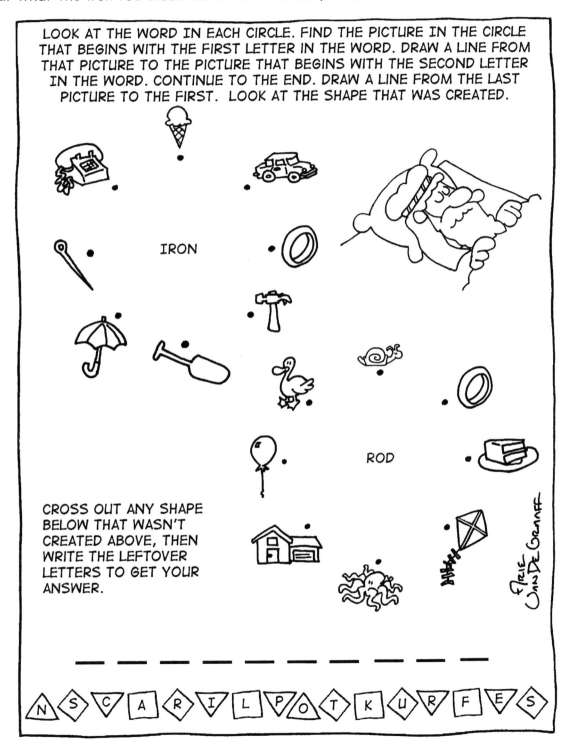

LOOK AT THE WORD IN EACH CIRCLE. FIND THE PICTURE IN THE CIRCLE THAT BEGINS WITH THE FIRST LETTER IN THE WORD. DRAW A LINE FROM THAT PICTURE TO THE PICTURE THAT BEGINS WITH THE SECOND LETTER IN THE WORD. CONTINUE TO THE END. DRAW A LINE FROM THE LAST PICTURE TO THE FIRST. LOOK AT THE SHAPE THAT WAS CREATED.

IRON

ROD

CROSS OUT ANY SHAPE BELOW THAT WASN'T CREATED ABOVE, THEN WRITE THE LEFTOVER LETTERS TO GET YOUR ANSWER.

N S C A R I L P O T K U R F E S

Joseph Smith's younger brother Samuel was the Church's first missionary. His efforts to share the Book of Mormon led to the baptism of Brigham Young and Heber C. Kimball, who became great leaders of the Church. Find ten differences between these pictures of Samuel Smith's first mission.

On an early morning in June 1830, Joseph Smith and other men built a dam on a stream so they could baptize several people, including Joseph's wife, Emma. They had to hurry because an angry mob wanted to stop the baptisms from taking place. Help Joseph Smith travel between the members of the mob without passing directly in front of one.

Jonah was an Old Testament prophet who was swallowed by a whale after he failed to obey a commandment from God. See if you can spot ten differences between these two pictures of Jonah.

In the Old Testament, Rebekah gave a great example of service. She graciously drew water from a well to provide drink for Abraham's servant and his ten camels. Find all the hidden objects in this picture of Rebekah at the well.

BANANA   BUTTERFLY   CELL PHONE   CUPCAKE   ENVELOPE   FEATHER   FISH   FORK

LOLLYPOP   NEEDLE   PAINTBRUSH   PEAR   PIE   SCREW   SOCK   WATCH

As members of the Church, we need to be obedient like Nephi was when the Lord commanded him to return to Jerusalem to get the brass plates. See if you can find ten things that don't belong in this picture.

In the Book of Mormon, the wicked people of Ammonihah imprisoned Alma and Amulek for many days. Then the Lord delivered them by causing an earthquake to destroy the prison. This story reminds us that Heavenly Father is always mindful of us. Find a path that will lead Alma and Amulek out of the rubble.

Daniel needs to make his way past the lions to the ladder and out of the lions' den. See if you can help him by taking a path that leads to the ladder without walking directly in front of a lion.

As members of the Church, we need to be courageous in standing up for what we believe, like David was. Now David needs your help. Which sling holds the rock David needs to defeat Goliath?

In the Book of Mormon, Helaman led an army of stripling warriors during a dangerous war with the Lamanites. These young warriors were known for their great faith. Can you find which two sets of stripling warriors are an exact match?

Each of these people is wearing or holding something in common with another. For example, Ammon has the same sling hanging from his belt as the thief right in front of him. Now find out what that thief has in common with another and so on, to discover what lesson these Lamanite thieves learned from Ammon when they tried to steal the king's sheep. It's a lesson we all need to know.

SECRET MESSAGE:

D O _ _ _ _   _ _ _ _ _ _

Prophets aren't the only things you can read about in the scriptures. A number of animals are mentioned in the scriptures and in Church history. See if you can match each prophet with an animal that plays a major role in his story.

In Ephesians 6:11–17, Paul describes the armor of God. Draw a line from each piece of armor to the New Testament-era soldier. Then draw a line to the young boy from each additional item that can help you today.

Captain Moroni raised the title of liberty to remind his people to stand up for the things they believed in. Today, we also need to stand up for the things we believe in. Find the hidden objects in this picture.

BANANA   CELL PHONE   CHEESE   CRAYON   DONUT   FORK   OLIVE   ORANGE

PENCIL   PICKLE   PIZZA   SAFETY PIN   TIE   TOOTH   WATCH   WATERMELON

Samuel the Lamanite showed great courage in standing up for what he believed, while facing wicked Nephites on the walls of Zarahemla. Help Samuel the Lamanite work his way past the evil Nephites without passing directly in front of a Nephite.

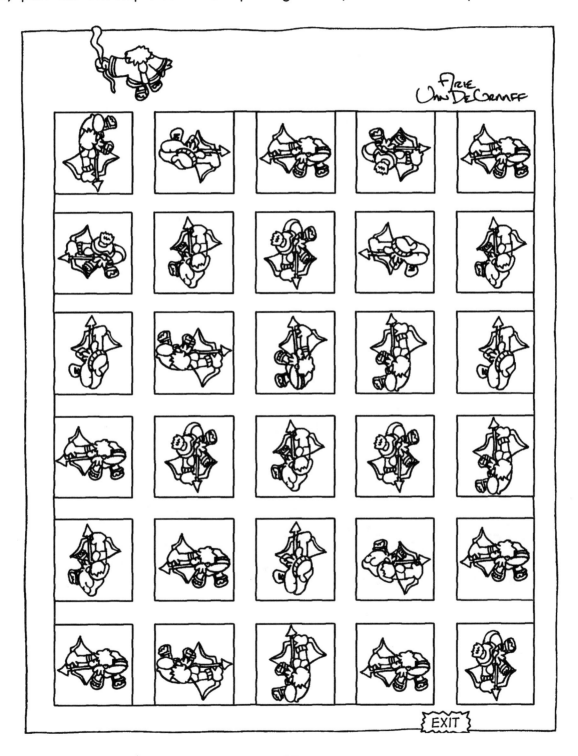

The early Saints in Utah spent forty years building the Salt Lake Temple. Patience is a characteristic we need as Church members today. Show your patience by figuring out where each jigsaw piece goes in this picture.

The Articles of Faith

IN 1842 THE PROPHET JOSEPH SMITH RESPONDED TO A REQUEST FROM A NEWSPAPER IN CHICAGO TO EXPLAIN THE BELIEFS OF THE CHURCH. IN HIS RESPONSE HE WROTE THE ARTICLES OF FAITH. NOW, THE ARTICLES OF FAITH ARE INCLUDED IN OUR SCRIPTURES, GIVING US A CLEAR UNDERSTANDING OF THE MAJOR BELIEFS OF THE CHURCH. HELP MOLLY DISCOVER IN WHICH BOOK OF SCRIPTURE THE ARTICLES OF FAITH ARE FOUND, BY USING THE CODE BELOW.

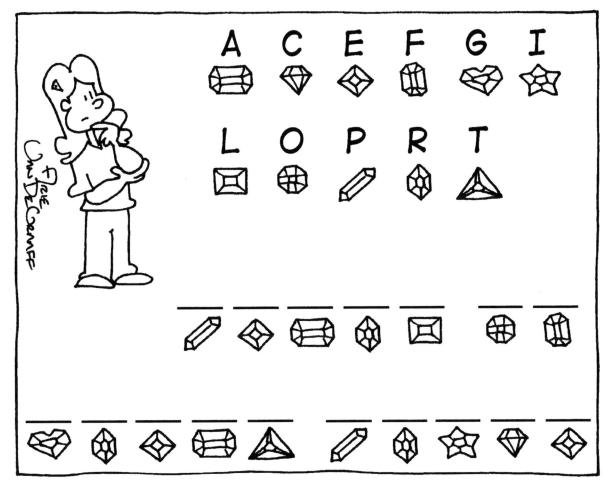

In Primary, Molly and Peter are learning about the Articles of Faith. The first article of faith teaches that we believe in God, the Eternal Father, and in His Son, Jesus Christ, and in the Holy Ghost. See if you can find the number 1 in this picture thirteen times.

The second article of faith teaches that we are not responsible for Adam's transgression. See if you can find ten differences between these two pictures of Adam and Eve leaving the Garden of Eden.

The third article of faith teaches how we are saved from our sins and mistakes. Follow the instructions below to find out which of Christ's gifts makes it possible to be saved.

MATCH THE SQUARES BELOW WITH THE SAME SQUARES IN THE PICTURE ABOVE. WRITE THE LETTERS FOR EACH SQUARE ON THE SPACE BELOW, THE LETTER ON THE SIDE FIRST AND THE LETTER ON TOP SECOND, TO GET YOUR ANSWER. (CAREFUL, SOME OF THE SQUARES ARE UPSIDE DOWN.)

A _ _ _ _ _ _ _ _ _ _

In the fourth article of faith, we learn that faith in the Lord Jesus Christ is the first principle of the gospel. To find out what the seed of faith can grow according to a popular Primary song, use the grid to redraw the mixed-up picture.

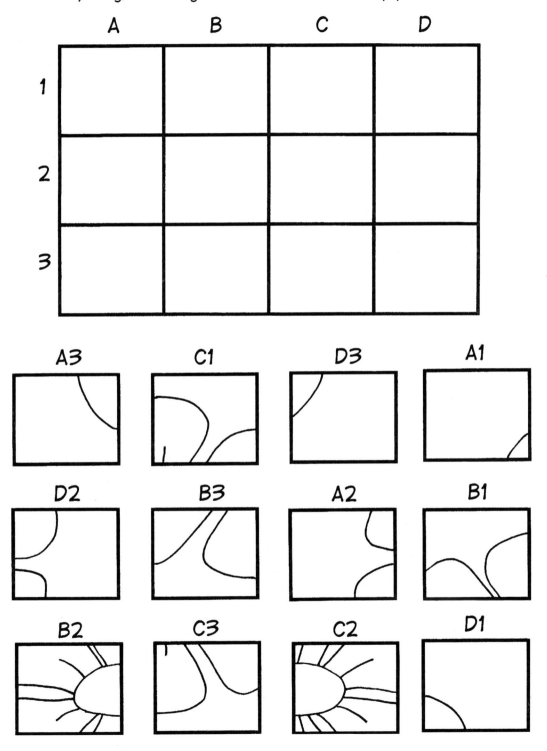

The fifth article of faith says that Church leaders must be called of God and that they must be ordained by those holding proper priesthood authority. See if you can find the two identical pictures.

The sixth article of faith says that we believe in the same organization of the Church that existed when Jesus Christ lived on the earth. See if you can find ten differences between these two pictures of Peter, James, and John.

According to the seventh article of faith, we believe in the gifts of the Spirit. Using the key below, figure out which gift of the Spirit allows these missionaries to speak a foreign language.

The eighth article of faith says we believe that the Bible and the Book of Mormon are the word of God. Draw a line from each scripture hero to the book that tells his story.

SAMSON

LEHI

PAUL

MORMON

HOLY BIBLE

Book OF MORMON

AMMON

MOSES

CAPTAIN MORONI

The ninth article of faith teaches that we believe in continued revelation. See if you can find the hidden images in this picture of Joseph Smith preaching.

BANANA   BUTTERFLY   CANDY CANE   FEATHER   FOOTBALL   HORSESHOE   PAINTBRUSH   PENCIL

PINE TREE   PIZZA SLICE   PUMPKIN   RAINBOW   RULER   TEACUP   WATERMELON   WRENCH

The tenth article of faith talks about missionary work throughout the world. Help these two missionaries as they prepare to go out into the world, by drawing a line from the objects they'll need to their suitcases (one of the objects will be needed by both missionaries).

The eleventh article of faith teaches that all people have the right to worship God however they choose. Find the path that will lead the family in this picture to their chapel for their Sunday meetings.

The twelfth article of faith says that Church members should honor the government of the country in which they live. These eight-year-old members of the Church live in countries all over the world. Follow each path to discover which country each child lives in.

The thirteenth article of faith says that Church members seek after anything that is virtuous, lovely, or of good report or praiseworthy. Help the girl find her way out of the lovely flower garden to her mother.

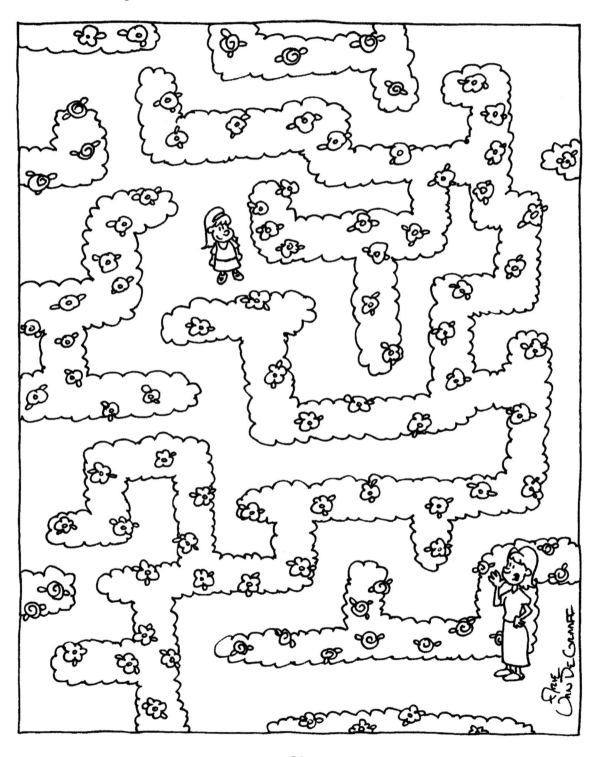

Missionary Work

MISSIONARIES THROUGHOUT THE WORLD BAPTIZE HUNDREDS OF THOUSANDS OF PEOPLE EVERY YEAR INTO THE CHURCH. EVERY ONE OF US SHOULD HELP THE MISSIONARIES BY BEING GOOD FRIENDS AND EXAMPLES TO THOSE AROUND US. WE HAVE A RESPONSIBILITY TO SHOW OTHERS HOW GOOD MEMBERS OF THE CHURCH SHOULD ACT. WHEN PETER GROWS A FOOT OR TWO, HE'LL SERVE A FULL-TIME MISSION. BEFORE THAT TIME, HE'LL NEED GOOD MISSIONARY SHOES. SEE IF YOU CAN FIND THE MATCHING PAIR OF SHOES BELOW.

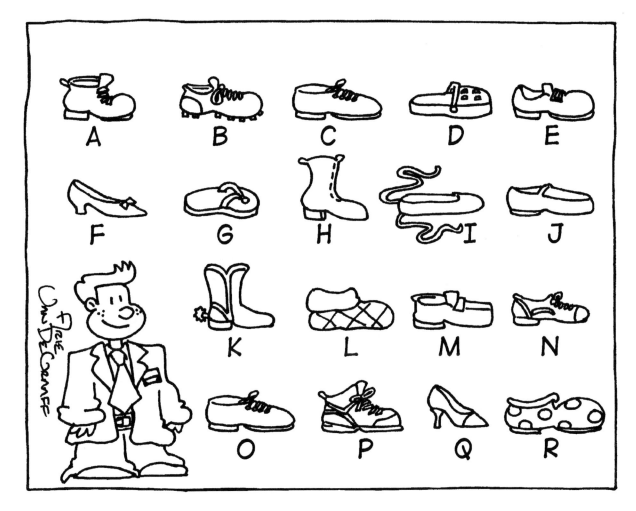

To find out what girls can do in eighteen months that takes boys twenty-four months to do, follow the directions below.

MATCH THE SQUARES BELOW WITH THE SAME SQUARES IN THE PICTURE ABOVE. WRITE THE LETTERS FOR EACH SQUARE ON THE SPACE BELOW, THE LETTER ON THE SIDE FIRST AND THE LETTER ON TOP SECOND, TO GET YOUR ANSWER. (CAREFUL, SOME OF THE SQUARES ARE UPSIDE DOWN.)

___ ___ ___ ___ ___ ___ ___ ___

These missionaries are packing their suitcases, but they'll need more than just clothes. Discover some characteristics these missionaries will need to bring with them by first identifying the missing letters and then unscrambling those missing letters into words.

Which path leads the missionaries to their investigator and his baptism appointment?

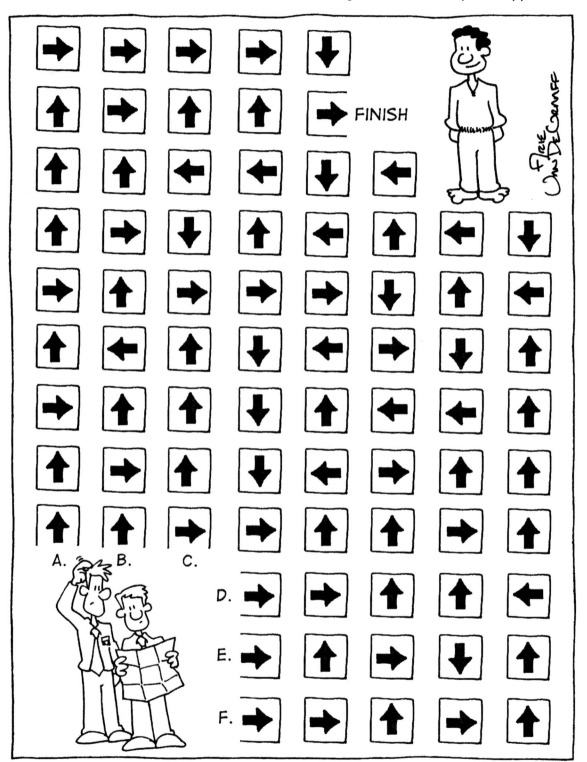

These missionaries just passed out their last copy of the Book of Mormon. See if you can find more copies for them. There are ten hidden Books of Mormon in this picture.

Each person in this picture has something in common with someone else in the picture. For example, the missionary on the left has the same backpack as a guy on the right side of the picture. Now find out what that guy has in common with another and so on, to discover what you can do to be like these missionaries.

SECRET MESSAGE:

B E _ _ _ _ _ _ _ _ _

These pictures of missionaries getting into a home to teach an investigator are all mixed up. In the upper left-hand corner of each picture, write the order (from 1 to 6) of the pictures in the story.

These sister missionaries are teaching a family about the gospel. See if you can find the hidden objects in the picture.

APPLE   BANANA   BASEBALL   BELL   BOWLING PIN   CANDLE   COMB   DONUT

FEATHER   HOT DOG   KITE   PEANUT   PENCIL   RULER   SCISSORS   WRENCH

Missionaries love dinner appointments. Can you find a clear path on the table for the missionaries to reach the pieces of cake?

The missionaries have a teaching appointment but don't remember the investigator's apartment number. Can you find the matching apartment?

Missionaries are always looking for investigators who will be a good match for the gospel of Jesus Christ. Which set of missionaries matches the set on the top of the page?

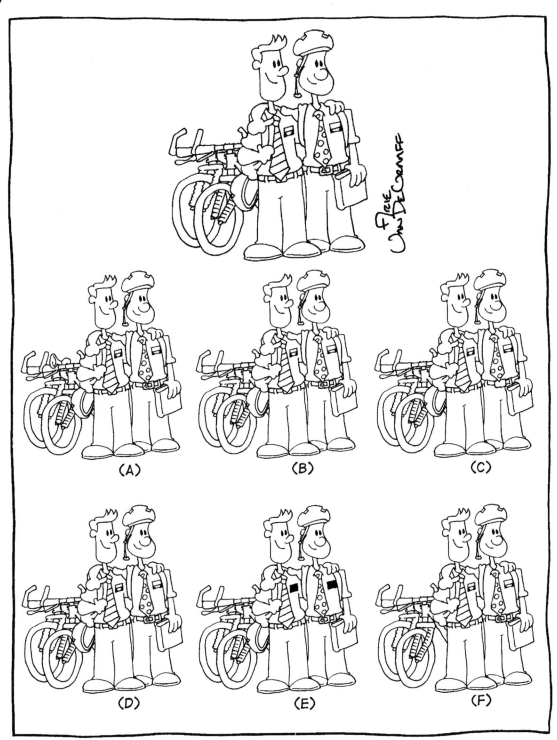

Answers

page 3
The eight things in common are: alarm clock, book, mug, pencil, picture of temple, plant, soccer ball, and trophy.

page 4
The ten differences between the two pictures are: balloon, bow, cake/cupcake, dog's spot, earring, hair clip, Peter's shirt, polka dot, straw, and tie.

page 5
The following things are in sets of eight: candles, chairs, cups, flowers, forks, girls, hats, plates, polka dots on present, presents, and stripes on cat.

page 6

page 7
A. watch, B. earrings, C. hat, D. tie, E. food, F. pets, G. glasses, H. balls

page 8
"Neighbor"

page 9
"Help Others"

page 10
"A Baptism"

page 11
"Polka Dot"

page 12

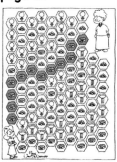

page 13

page 14
"Practice"

page 15
"Baptism"

page 16
Seating Order: 1. Dad, 2. Mom, 3. Will, 4. Ty, 5. Ava, 6. Tess, 7. Leah, 8. Gabe

page 17
"Uncle Joel"

page 18

page 19
The ten differences between the two pictures are: boy's jacket, father's hair, hair clip, mirror, partition latch, pigtail/ponytail, scriptures, tie, tile, and vest.

page 20
"Comforter"

page 21
"Service"

page 22

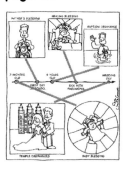

page 23
The program for Primary girls who have turned eight is Activity Days.

page 24

page 25

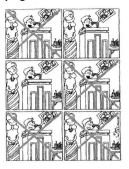

page 26
"Testimonies"

page 27
"Tithing"

page 28
"B" and "F" are the matching dinners.

page 29
House "O" is where the deacons need to go.

page 30
From left to right: R.S. president, deacon, bishop, chorister, and missionary

page 31
The ten differences between the two pictures are: banana/apple, bow, clock, fork/spoon, glasses, hair, lunch bag, sandwich, straw, and stripe on shirt.

page 32

page 33

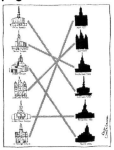

page 34
"Hold Firm"

page 34
"Commandments"

page 36
The ten things wrong are: dog's feet, end table's feet, fish with remote control, flippers, hot dogs on tree, outerspace in window, paintbrush, pan on head, upside-down lamp, and upside-down picture.

page 37
"Repent"

page 38

page 39

page 40

page 41

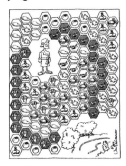

page 42

page 43

page 44
A. sash, B. sword, C. satchel, D. head band, E. staff, F. beard, G. arrow, H. plates

page 45

page 46

page 47
"Book of Mormon"

page 48

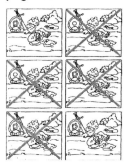

page 49
The ten things wrong with this picture are: alarm clock, baseball hat, basketball, candy bar, flashlight, MP3 player, pencil, pennant, pizza, and poster.

page 50
The order from left to right, top to bottom, is: 5, 3, 6, 1, 2, 4.

page 51
"Scriptures"

page 52
The ten differences between the two pictures are: axe, bird, brim of hat, door handle, jacket button, pig, satchel clasp, suspender clips, tree, and wheat.

page 53

page 54
The ten differences between the two pictures are: beach ball, crab, direction of duck, drip of water, fish, Jonah's beard, knot on wood, piece of cloth, stripe on robe, and whale's ribs.

page 55

page 56
The ten things wrong with this picture are: baseball hat, bicycle, cell phone, cup with straw, satellite dish, soccer ball, sneakers, sunglasses, watch, and wrench.

page 57

page 58

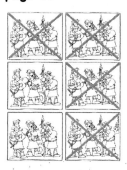

page 59
Sling B

page 60

page 61
"Do Not Steal"

page 62

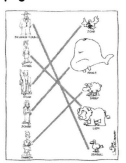

page 63

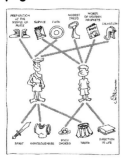

page 64

page 65

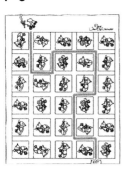

page 66
From left to right: B, A, D, C

page 67
"Pearl of Great Price"

page 68

page 69
The ten differences between the two pictures are: belt, berry, bird's beak, bunny and dog, bush, flower, fruit, rock, sandals, and tree branch.

page 70
"Atonement"

page 71

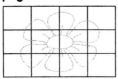

page 72

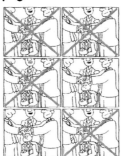

page 73
The ten differences between the two pictures are: button on shirt, dog's tongue, fish in basket, fish on line, hand on shoulder, palm tree, sandal, sash, stripe on robe, and tree branch.

page 74
"Gift of Tongues"

page 75

page 76

page 77

page 78
"C" is the correct route to the church building.

page 79
From left to right: Australia, Slovenia, Austria, Japan, and Nigeria

page 80

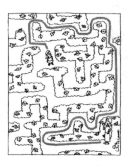

page 81
"C" and "O" are the matching shoes.

page 82
"A mission"

page 83
"Faith" and "Courage"

page 84
"F" is the correct route to the investigator.

page 85

page 86
"Be an example"

page 87
The order from left to right, top to bottom is: 5, 4, 2, 6, 1, 3.

page 88

page 89

page 90
Door 303.

page 91
"D" is the matching missionary pair.